The Secret Cornell

by

Doug Baird

Table of Contents

Copyright Page 1

The Secret Cornell 5

Introduction 6

Fraudulent Policies 7

Unilateral Planning 8

"Cooperative" Planning 9

Cornell Paranoia 10

Subverting Town Law 11

Urban Colonialism 12

Lack of Public Participation 13

Cornell's Rural Planning 16

Cornell Takes Charge 17

Cornell's Expansion 20

Cornell's Rural Planning 21

Cornell's Coronation 23

Cornell's "Rural Humanities" 24

The Destruction of Rural Lansing..25

The Importance of Being Cornell 27

Scurvy Survey 30

Doubling up on Double-talk..32

"Rural Sprawl" and Expansionism..35

Form-Based Dictatorship..37

"Importance" is Everything..38

A matter of Form 40

"Complete" Rubbish..42

NYSDEC + TMDL = Business as Usual..45

All Roads Lead to Cornell 46

Rural Road Trip..49

Deadly Drift..52

Non-Disclosure Policy..55

Runaround 60

In Conclusion..62

Epilogue..63

What does being the poorest, most marginalized, and most unrepresented group of people in Tompkins County make you?

The perfect victim.

Introduction

It's not surprising that a world-class university like Cornell and the uber-powerful agricultural lobby can combine to thoroughly crush the most marginalized and unrepresented sector of New York State's population. It's also not surprising that no one is willing to stand up for us.

When Cornell's rural policy planner publicly stated that no one but farmers "deserved to live there," she helped lay the groundwork for Tompkins County's most recent "vision of the future": one in which the present rural community no longer exists.

With an elitist policymaking that has closer ties to the Khmer Rouge than the Constitution, Tompkins County is a college destination with the sort of moral compass that lands people a spot on American Greed.

What is The Secret Cornell?

It's a betrayal of trust that makes the College Admissions Scandal seem like throat-clearing at a political rally.

There's much more to this story than I am putting in this book. It's a story that would open the door to shocking revelations, but it's who's behind that door that keeps politicians and the media from ever turning the knob.

Fraudulent Policies

Where should I start? If Tompkins County's policies are not outright lies, they are certainly fraudulent.

The county's policymaking is a Jenga of misrepresentations, of cunningly shaped arguments that are held together by power, cronyism, and corruption working together to prevent the removal of any piece that would bring about its collapse. There is no meaningful public participation — just the repeated assertion that there is.

Policies are released to the public with the trumpeting of a proclamation, and the "take it, or leave it, but there's nothing you can do about it" smugness of plans well laid by superior intellects.

Tompkins County is a college-controlled class system with many levels, the lowest being occupied by the rural poor. Rural people are considered to be of such little worth that planners don't even speak with the rural communities that their policies directly impact. We are openly treated like the evicted tenants of the Irish landlords: as disposable goods. And when you're disposable, you can't be a victim.

Unilateral Planning

People say, "You can't pull yourself up by your bootstraps," but Cornell's rural policies are made and ratified without any participation or representation by the county's rural residents, and built upon with no more legitimacy than their bureaucratic approval. This creates a planning portfolio that maximizes Cornell's profits on the backs of a poor and despised rural population.

It's elitist planning on a level that is so protected from debate that not only does Cornell promote an urban sprawl bedroom community in rural Lansing, their planning groups insist that the only solution is to bulldoze more rural green spaces to greatly increase its size and density, and create an urban node. Blaming the town's rural community for this "rural sprawl" problem.

And it's through the flagrant abuse of Cornell's corporate and political power that these rural policies can never be questioned, publicly debated, or even written about, so that they will never need to be defended.

"Cooperative" Planning

Tompkins County's "cooperative planning" is a concept created by Cornell to legitimize unilateral policymaking for their sole benefit.

Cornell's planners cite "agriculture" as a banner cry for their mistreatment of the vast majority of those living in rural Lansing. Even though the area was settled more than 200 years ago, all non-farming rural residents are now demonized as squandering natural resources and restricting the activities of invasive Concentrated Animal Feeding Operations (CAFOs), who rule this unilaterally created agricultural zone without hindrance. It's these land-gobbling farms that spearhead Cornell's urban colonialism in rural New York.

And just as the Irish landlords exported shipload after shipload of food to England at the height of the Irish famine, Cornell's rich CAFOs and agribusiness partners promote policies that remove all services and land uses from the rural poor while increasing taxes and assessments on rural communities that are already dying from crime, drugs, and neglect.

Cornell's planning policies regularize a constructive eviction that is eroding the county's rural communities like a flood of toxic waste.

Cornell Paranoia

Like the first faint whiff of putrescence, there is a sheen of anxiety that coats the activities of those in College Town, born of the need to always conform: "Cornell Paranoia."

Ithaca is not a welcoming place. It's a place where non-conforming thoughts are not welcome, where visitors are asked their reason for being there. A place where your adherence to doctrine is casually checked within the first few sentences of a social meeting — and everything depends on it.

I first heard of Cornell Paranoia from a blogger describing her fear to write about, or even link to, my work. She told me that she was afraid her bosses would find out and she would lose her job. Cornell Paranoia was uttered with a fragile smile.

Cornell is not a beacon of enlightenment. It's a centrality of power, and the county's battered rural community bears the marks of its well-used club.

Subverting Town Law

Legality, legitimacy, ethics, and the intent of New York State Town Law have little meaning in Tompkins County. Although Town Law states, "Among the most important powers and duties granted by the legislature to a town government is the authority and responsibility to undertake town comprehensive planning," the Town of Lansing Comprehensive Plan was created and approved by Cornell for corporate profit. And while Town Law's intent was that the comprehensive plan "is in the best interest of the people of each town," Cornell's planners ignored and subverted that intent, overturning Lansing's best interest, and claiming the law "does not forbid a more coordinated process." They even called their self-serving, predatory policymaking a "symbiotic relationship."

The planning began with Cornell's Survey Research Institute cold calling about the issues (before Lansing residents even knew they were issues) and ended with a comprehensive plan that was never allowed to be publicly questioned, debated, or approved by the town's residents.

No authority, at any level, will admit to oversight or jurisdiction, or has shown any willingness to help Lansing's residents. Cornell owns Tompkins County.

Urban Colonialism

Cornell University, like other colonial powers, quells unrest at home through the application of foreign booty. Whatever happens in the rest of Tompkins County is of no interest to the dwellers of Ithaca. Newspapers and social media froth in a teapot of narcissistic navel viewing, hair-splitting doctrinal reasoning, and witch-hunting the scent of non-conformity.

Cornell's urban colonialist policies maintain a constant flow, exporting problems and burdens to rural towns, and skimming a higher quality of life for Ithacans, who are still able to feel a pea of discomfort through the many layers of perks and privileges. Cornell planners promote a society of dependence at home, supported by taxation and privation abroad.

Even the industrial policies echo those of past colonial paradigms. When the Town of Lansing was about to receive natural gas from New York State Electric and Gas (NYSEG) and attract business and manufacturing, Cornell's county legislature traveled to Albany to block it. In Tompkins County's planning documents, it clearly states that Ithaca is to be the center of business, industry, finance, and culture . . . the center of all. The centrality.

Lack of Public Participation

A "distinction without a difference" is the best way to describe the political orientation of the government in Tompkins County. It's obviously a dictatorship, but whether it's fascist, socialist, progressive, or colonialist is of little importance to those who suffer at its dictates.

Cornell's leadership position in the "centrality" of New York seems to add an overlay of patrician arrogance to their policymaking rhetoric. Their arguments, instead of offering evidence, always assume that everything they say is beyond questioning, and they simply repeat their conclusions.

The following excerpts are from the Tompkins County Comprehensive Plan's "Listening to Community Voices":

> *A total of 915 responses were received either on-line or via written survey. A large number of written surveys were received as part of an outreach effort to Participation in Government classes at Ithaca High School, Lansing High School, Newfield High School, and New Roots Charter School.*

> *Another major public outreach effort was made in the spring of 2014 to receive input on the draft principles and policies for the Comprehensive Plan. Over 70 individuals attended the public meetings and additional comments were received via mail and email.*

Public comments:

> *Efforts to acquaint citizens with this plan which will, by design, touch each and every resident of Tompkins County are pitiful to non-existent. There were 4 meetings attended by a total of 70 individuals out of a Tompkins County population of 101,570.*
>
> *In a survey to critique the TC Plan conducted in the fall of 2013 there were 915 responses of .9% of the county population. Of these, a large number [more than 25%] were from Participation in Government classes in four local high schools. The session with Planning Department officials I attended earlier this month in the TC Library also seemed poorly attended. This is a laughable attempt at having an informed electorate.*

The county's response:

> *Listening to Community Voices describes the considerable efforts to involve the public at three separate stages in preparing the Comprehensive Plan.*

The county's beliefs are always correct, their policies are always beneficial, the involvement of the public is always sufficient — and they never change anything.

While most governments are vulnerable to public opinion and wary of public outcry, Cornell's crony conglomerate has no fear of anyone upsetting the applecart. They are a world-class influencer in the middle of an unimportant rural electorate, with the land-grant seat of America's agricultural overlords and the in-their-pocket representation of 30,000 uncaring students, all implemented by a lock-step legislature that accedes to every word and hint.

It's a government whose professed social beliefs can only be of importance to academic quibblers, not to the rural poor they rob and repress.

Cornell, Ithaca College, and the county's corporations and institutions are locked together in a public love-embrace (and a private share-out) of policymaking and profiting — a fountain of eternal use spilling into a privatization of the public trust.

Ithaca is an oasis in the desert of New York's rural poverty — a gated community for members only.

Cornell's Rural Planning

When I call Tompkins County's policymaking fraudulent, it's not just mud throwing; their actions fit the legal definition of fraud.

So why isn't anybody doing anything about it?

Because politicians have set the value of our human worth at keeping Cornell happy.

Cornell's quid-pro cronyism of interlocking corporations, institutions, and powerful interests is the model for a centrality that is sucking the last bit of profit from between the weaves of our unraveling society. There is no one left to turn to.

In Tompkins County, fraud is not an isolated issue. It's coupled with every kind of ethical and legal misconduct that any authority can commit, from refusing to follow the regulations and intent of New York State Town Law and ignoring the Best Practices of the American Planning Association to creating policies that are unconscionable contracts written by authorities in a position of public trust.

And there is not one fact, action, or county planning "vision" that contradicts this statement.

It's a perfect circumstantial case that no one wants to bring to court.

Cornell Takes Charge

Your actions define you, and it's fraud, misconduct, and cronyism that defines Tompkins County's planners and policy makers.

Self-interest is the basis of every Cornell planned policy, and the raison d'être of the county's authorities.

THE TOMPKINS COUNTY COMPREHENSIVE PLAN presents a vision for the future of the community. It is based on a set of principles that reflect the values of the community as expressed by the County Legislature they have elected. The Plan seeks to foster a place where individual rights are protected while recognizing the benefits that can accrue to community members from common actions. It largely focuses on voluntary collaboration between the public and private sectors, but also supports the role that local regulation can play in addressing key issues impacting the entire community and helping people to live together in harmony. Where regulation is required, it should balance the burdens placed on individuals and businesses with the restrictions needed to protect or otherwise benefit the larger community. In most cases the Plan seeks to expand individual choice in terms of where and how people live their lives.

At first glance, Cornell's Tompkins County "vision" reads like a visitor center brochure, but a more thorough inspection reveals authoritarian boot marks among the carefully worded phrases.

- It reflects the "values of the community" — but only "as expressed by the County Legislature."
- It claims to "foster a place where individual's rights are protected" — but in the same sentence subordinates them to "common actions."
- It "focuses on voluntary" — but "supports the role of local regulation."

And while the county's plan states, "Where regulation is required, it should balance the burdens placed on individuals and businesses with the restrictions needed to protect or otherwise benefit the larger community," it indicates nowhere that there will be any public participation in what these regulations and burdens are — or how they will be implemented.

By removing those portions of this "vision" statement that are negated by qualifiers, we arrive at a more straightforward disclosure of intent:

This plan is based on values that reflect the principles of the county's legislature. In serving this agenda, we will choose what burdens we will place on individuals and businesses, and decide whom we will restrict in their choice of where and how they can live.

The Tompkins County Comprehensive Plan is as compassionate as putting a flowered border on a foreclosure notice.

"In rural areas the Plan envisions a working landscape of farms and forests."

In the county's "vision for the future," the rural community no longer exists.

Cornell's Expansion

While Cornell's comprehensive plan for Tompkins County readily admits that "New York State clearly places land use authority in the hands of its towns, villages, and cities," it urges local municipalities to renounce that duty by offering local bureaucrats an easier job for the same pay:

"Often, local municipalities have a full workload simply addressing the important day-to-day issues of local concern. Planning at the county level can help municipal governments address key issues of concern that cross municipal boundaries."

Expressing concern and offering to help by taking control is a classic subterfuge in expanding a government's power — that government being Cornell.

This directly contradicts the "legislative findings and intent" of New York Town Law — that a town government should "assure full opportunity for citizen participation in the preparation of such proposed plan."

Throwing the baby out with the bath water merely gives Cornell a clean basin to fill with their pickings and clears a path for Lansing's "form-based" future. A future without the rural community.

Cornell's Rural Planning

You're a world-class university corporation that is always seeking to expand. And you despise the poor rural people that surround you, but you covet their land.

What do you do after you've taken away all their participation and worth?

You take away their freedom.

In the Tompkins County "rich farmer — poor non-farmer" equation, there is no attempt at equitable treatment. Cornell's "urban colonialist" government has passed restriction after restriction on Lansing's 200-year old rural community — agricultural law has replaced administrative law, and corruption has replaced conscience.

In 2023, Lansing's "Vichy" government "expressly repealed and superseded" the existing rural/agricultural zoning, replacing it with a punitive agricultural zoning. This new zoning unilaterally stripped sixty-four previously permitted rural land uses — even those "permitted as of right" — from 95% of the population and "streamlined" the approval of all agricultural uses.

This manifest abuse of zoning power left the non-farming rural residents with just four permitted uses: one- and two-unit dwellings, a bed and breakfast, or a day-care facility. This zoning policy forces all large parcels into the hands of expanding corporate CAFOs or leaves them exposed to a predatory tax structure.

In recent years, Cornell's takeover of Lansing's government, their promotion of urban sprawl planning, and the proliferation of suburban developments have radically changed this once-rural town. The new agricultural zone is just one more step in the constructive eviction of Lansing's rural community.

Tompkins County isn't a representative government; it's a gang. The Cornell gang.

Cornell's Coronation

There's a trail left by Cornell's planning on the county's rural communities; it's a serpentine path that is anything but meandering. Sometimes it pushes against the boundaries of license, and sometimes it caresses the shackles of repression, but it always follows the path of greatest profit.

In a self-serving new millennium way, Cornell molds particles of fact and law together to create a reasoning that was never intended — to legitimize their policies of unilateral gain.

Cornell's planners talk about working together, but theirs is not the together of equals. It's the together of master and servant, or master and slave. There is no togetherness in Cornell's "together" — it's a leadership by elitist proclamation and enforcement by tax collector and bailiff.

From cap and gown to robe and crown, Cornell typifies the trend of our country's progressive elite: from thinking they're better than other people to acting on that belief.

Cornell's "Rural Humanities"

How do you value an educator who has no value for anyone else's ideas?

If you were to put the response of Tompkins County's college authorities to rural justice questions into categories, the largest category would be "not answering." In fifteen years of sending books, emails, and letters, I have received only one response in my search for rural social justice, telling me that the concept of rural people being marginalized and excluded comes from those who "lived in simpler times."

It's revealing that Cornell's Rural Humanities focuses on stories of LGBTQIA+ and Black lives, ignoring the plight of the county's rural residents and reinforcing their tacit approval of the college's "rural repressive" planning policies.

The question of these educators acting to expose rural poverty and marginalization is buffered with silence and denial — in stark contrast to the *inexcusable* and *unacceptable* labels they readily apply to any city-centric issue.

In collegiate Tompkins County, overarching policies have progressed to all-controlling ones — and only doctrinal "fact gathering" is allowed.

The Destruction of Rural Lansing

If you ask Lansing's town government to do anything for the rural community, they ignore you. And if you ask them again, you're a troublemaker.

Their denial of the worth of Lansing's rural residents is not just a passive thing; they actively refuse to respond to or acknowledge anything that comes from the rural community. Letters, emails, and documents disappear into the town's offices, and whether they are even opened and read is left to the imagination.

In contrast, their reaction to Cornell-connected agricultural interests is almost fawning. I was there a few years ago when a farmer strode into a town meeting, announcing that a landowner who rented to him had signed a much more lucrative lease with a solar farm company. Within days, the town board released a public policy statement condemning that action, and created a bureaucratic atmosphere of obstruction and denial for solar farm land usage.

More recently, when farmers submitted a unilateral restructuring of rural land to the Town of Lansing, removing almost every allowed non-farming rural land use and "streamlining" the approval of all agriculture uses, there was no representation or participation by the town's rural community and no debate. This exclusionary rezoning plan was quickly passed without demur.

Cornell's progressive government practices a de facto rural segregation as rigid as any racial one in our history.

In Lansing's recent "loophole election" (in which Cornell's Vichy government won every town board seat), not one of these Cornell-affiliated candidates visited or had anything to do with the town's rural community. Instead, they gerrymandered a voting advantage by using a loophole that allowed residents of a neighboring suburban municipality to vote in Lansing town elections, putting up yard signs urging them to vote.

The Importance of Being Cornell

If you listed all the actions that Cornell's policymakers and the Cornell-controlled Tompkins County government have taken against the rural community, it would mirror those that despots and bigots have always used in targeting the people they hate and plunder. In New York State, agricultural law steps beyond any pretense of equality to treat the existing rural population as unwelcome interlopers who (as a Cornell Cooperative Extension policy writer publicly proclaimed) "don't deserve to live there." This lawmaking bias is further supported by giving New York State's commissioner of agriculture and markets the ability to intimidate and compel local governments to remove anything that he decides "unreasonably restricts farm operations," as well as the power to define a farm operation: "The New York State Court of Appeals has consistently ruled that these orders are entitled to administrative deference in the interpretation and administration of this important right to farm protection."

It's worth adding to the list of policy biases that New York State, Tompkins County, and the Town of Lansing all use the word "important" whenever agricultural interests are mentioned, but not for anything else in the rural community, including the health and well-being of its poor and disposable families.

(I've already written about how the Lansing Town Board unilaterally rubber-stamped a farmers' zoning plan to strip the non-farming rural residents of almost every land usage they were traditionally permitted.)

The county's rural residents are vilified repeatedly in planning documents as the ones who "restrict farming," are destroying farmlands with "rural sprawl," and are depleting natural resources through actions such as their use of well water. With the combination of ignorance and arrogance that is the hallmark of collegiate Ithaca, the county's elite only know what they're told, and they're willing to do anything on that basis.

The facts, however, reveal these assertions to be pure propaganda. The Cornell-written Lansing Agriculture Protection Plan states, "Farming is alive and well in the Town of Lansing." It never once mentions any restrictions or any attempts to restrict agriculture by the rural community, who are far too poor and powerless to have any influence at all on the activities of these rich corporate farms.

"Rural sprawl" is a term created by Cornell planners to obfuscate an agenda of unrestricted "urban sprawl" in the south of Lansing, while in the north of town, all authority was given over to Cornell's agribusiness affiliates. The lakeshore, scraped clean of locals, has become an enclave of Cornell's rich.

Rural Lansing's residents pay the same tax rates as every other county resident but get no services. County policy denies us any municipal water, any municipal sewers, and any mass transit, and the sheriff's department only comes to write a report.

Cornell's policies of promoting rural land-hungry CAFOs, along with upscale urban sprawl development, skyrocketing assessments, and a high-tax bedroom community school district, are constructively evicting the poor rural residents out of their homes and out of the county. I can't even say, "Stop Cornell's policies and planning — they're destroying rural Lansing!" because they've already destroyed it and are moving on to another rural area they can "help."

Scurvy Survey

At the opposite end of the spectrum from all those business and product surveys that seek your opinion are the Cornell justification surveys.

These surveys are always taken after the policies and regulations have been privately decided, but before the residents are aware of them, so there can be no discussion or thinking things through beforehand. The data collection makes use of an accepted methodology to give legitimacy to its skewed and deceptive questions.

Cornell's cold-call "Lansing" telephone survey instituted a quota of respondents for each different demographic they had created, and hung up any anybody who had been "apportioned out."

The survey's psychologically manipulative questions didn't ask, "Would you support re-zoning to allow large-scale apartment complexes?" Instead, they asked, "Would you support housing for families in need?"

They asked what residents wanted in the town center, but never asked residents if they wanted a town center, allowing planners to claim that "residents wanted a town center with ___."

In the days following the survey, there was a ground swell of public unrest.

The Town of Lansing telephone survey's public meeting filled the town hall with angry and concerned residents. Authorities backed down, claiming that this survey was "only preliminary" and just "to get an indication," and that other surveys would be conducted later.

They lied.

No other surveys were ever conducted, and that same publicly rejected survey was presented unchanged throughout the Town of Lansing Comprehensive Plan as a public mandate.

In a university community notable for their intellectual dishonesty, the only wrongdoing is not getting what you want.

Doubling up on Double-talk

The Town of Lansing's Comprehensive Plan has all the fact-based believability of *Chariots of the Gods.*

New York State Town Law § 272-a clearly states:

"The development and enactment by the town government of a town comprehensive plan which can be readily identified, and is available for use by the public, is in the best interest of the people of each town."

The approved version of the Town of Lansing Comprehensive Plan substitutes a very different government policy:

"The best way to plan for the long-term future of the Town of Lansing is to decide regionally where the major commercial, educational, shopping, recreational, health care, agricultural, manufacturing and residential sectors will be located. The reality is that our municipalities are not in competition with each other; rather they survive in symbiotic relationships. We should build upon these cooperative relationships in land use decisions as well, while respecting a town's right to home rule. New York State Law delegates planning decisions to the town and city levels but does not forbid a more coordinated process."

However, in comparison with the other comprehensive plan in the county, *every other municipality in the county subordinates regional decisions to the best interests of that municipality.*

Cornell's relationship with the Town of Lansing is not a "symbiotic" one. It's predatory, and any claim of "cooperation" is belied by the creation of a comprehensive plan without any meaningful participation by Lansing's rural community. It's a plan that expunges the rural residents from its pages while forcing a runaway urban sprawl development that every other comprehensive plan pledges to avoid.

Cornell University's Survey Research Institute, Cornell Cooperative Extension, and Cornell Design Connect are the triumvirate who rule Lansing's future — supported, of course, by Cornell-led studies and planning groups.

There is not one "Town of Lansing" policy that was not designed by Cornell — and not one of these policies had any meaningful public participation or oversight by the town's residents.

The Town of Lansing Comprehensive Plan states, "The Town of Lansing has an extensive history, dating back to the conclusion of the Revolutionary War. Settled in 1791, Lansing began as an agricultural community . . ." and there, the history of the rural community stops. The next two hundred years of growth and social change are entirely unreported. More than 95% of the residents in the portion of Lansing that Cornell has carved out for CAFOs are not involved in agriculture. But the walls that imprison them are more than just corrupt and unilateral zoning decisions. Like the Berlin Wall, it divides Lansing between those who have freedom and those who are oppressed: a rural community whose individual rights and very existence are denied by the planners of Lansing's future.

It's a Cornell-written form-based plan that presents a vision of Lansing as one-part "bucolic" corporate CAFOs, and one-part "rural character" urban node housing — with the mansions of rich lakeshore incomers replacing the tax and code evicted locals.

And every policy in the Lansing Comprehensive Plan is "legitimized" by citing the same publicly rejected survey that the comprehensive plan writers claimed would never be used.

The Town of Lansing Comprehensive Plan is a meaningless babble of double-talk surrounding Cornell's agenda of displacing the existing rural community and resettling the town for their own use — creating a Vichy local government to enact repressive and marginalizing policies that they can't publicly defend.

"Rural Sprawl" and Expansionism

If it's true that history repeats itself, then so do the means used to legitimize a government's self-serving and repressive policymaking. That's why the term "rural sprawl" was coined to propagandize a fatuous domino effect scenario of a rural community "destroying our agricultural land."

There is an old joke about Cornell's "centrally located in New York" recruitment blurb: Cornell, centrally located in the middle of nowhere. This has been the albatross that Cornell's student and staff recruiters have had to deal with. How do you compete with the urban energy and access to culture and variety that other colleges can provide? By offering something they can't — a mid-century small town feeling, surrounded by parks and outdoor recreation.

Visitors marvel at this "small town" city, a place that they didn't think could still exist — because it doesn't. It's a form-based fallacy that hides the downside of Cornell's greedy corporate agenda: bulldozing fields, cutting down woods, and building thousands of new housing units in the once-rural community of Lansing, miles away, while doubling their benefit by bringing in new businesses and institutions and putting the high cost of services for their workers' families in Lansing — a different taxation district. Lansing, NY is now ruled by a grab-and-go policymaking that maximizes the short-term family benefits and property values of a "use and move" bedroom community that cares nothing for the town's past — or its future.

Unsurprisingly, the Tompkins County Comprehensive Plan does not mention "urban sprawl" even once — replacing it with exhortations to combat rural sprawl by "concentrating growth in the Development Focus Areas" and building high-density urban node housing (with the required infrastructure) in Lansing.

Cornell is moving into the future by reinventing the privileged elite of the past. Best planning practices have transitioned into "professionals in the service of profit," and public participation has been reduced to hearing what's already been decided.

Form-Based Dictatorship

Government authorities in Tompkins County are very careful about how they word official documents. They try to present a façade of whole community participation, while their planners use a "greater good" wrapping to muffle the sound of rural families being beaten into submission.

The once-rural Town of Lansing is no longer a place where neighborly attitudes are infused in a first-name group of town officials. Rural residents must now appeal to a stone-faced tribunal of Cornell incomers who, at every request, turn to the town's lawyer to support the legality of their denials.

"Participation" is a word that is only used in conjunction with existing programs—programs that are thoroughly under government control. "Input" is the preferred term for any public involvement in new planning issues, defining residents as the contributors to those who act, without any power to act as decisionmakers themselves.

It's laughable that Cornell's Design Connect uses "participation" more times in presenting their form-based codes than in all the other comprehensive plan pages combined, never once revealing that this authoritarian planning tool will strip residents of all meaningful participation and power.

The Town of Lansing's recent 312-page comprehensive plan is a planning document for the subjugation of rural Lansing, lengthily propagandizing the policies and restrictions of Cornell's urban colonialism as "the way we all must live."

"Importance" is Everything

The Town of Lansing Comprehensive Plan represents a convergence of "important" interests.

Lansing's most recent comprehensive plan uses the word "important" fifty-seven times, and almost half of these relate to agriculture – "Agriculture continues to remain important to the Town of Lansing," "Agriculture is important to the Town," "Agriculture is immensely important" — a self-written announcement of "importance" that rolls on and on, a victory monument to the rural ascendency of Cornell's College of Agriculture and their cooperative extension.

The existence of Lansing's long-established non-farming rural majority is expunged from the town's comprehensive plan.

The remaining labels of importance are used for Cornell's urban node resettlement, and support the aims, uses, and concern with resale values of a millennial grab-and-go bedroom community: schools are important, recreation is important, municipal water and sewers are important, mass transportation is important, and of course, "The most important regional connections are those that lead to Ithaca."

This rejection of a rural identity is further documented when the Comprehensive Plan "looks for the best strategies to strengthen local economic performance," stating that "it is important to focus on STEM (Science, Technology, and Engineering & Math) occupations because they are among the highest paying, fastest growing and most influential in driving economic growth and innovation." It thus embraces a cross-section of jobs that mirrors the skills of Cornell incomers and deliberately excludes the much less educated rural residents that this plan seeks to displace.

The "greater good" has given way to "importance" — an importance that not only demands recognition but counts everything and everyone else as unimportant. Lansing's rural poor have been consigned to unimportance through the influence of powerful and "important" agricultural and collegiate interests: the rural community's very existence remains unmentioned in planning documents — even in the policies that target and marginalize them.

The Town of Lansing Comprehensive Plan is blatantly elitist policymaking driven by what they hold to be most "important" — themselves.

A matter of Form

Cornell's planners are using form-based codes to remold the Town of Lansing, and its rural residents are just excess material.

The package presented by Cornell's Design Connect presents form-based codes as a gooey community-friendly confection with an enlightened functionality. But the contents of the box are quite different: an unyielding, unalterable centrality. With form-based codes, the only legally empowered participant is your government, and they retain all the decision-making power.

Only twenty-five residents attended the indifferently advertised form-based code meeting, and their attendance was of as little importance as their comments.

The presentation wasn't given to inform a decision-making public — it was a show-and-tell intended to check the "public participation" box. A puppet show of "form-based" authority.

The examples and arguments they used were only superficially convincing. A number of these plans had not even been implemented, and all were about increasing development — not preserving a rural town and a rural way of life.

While these form-based codes were slid into town planning with minimal public awareness, they loomed large in the comprehensive plan: "form-based" appeared eighty-five times and in conjunction with every new land use policy. And the plan's "Future Land Use" chapter is headed by "form-based tools," rapturously describing how they would encourage a "sense of community among neighbors" and insisting that "significant public input ensures that the impacted community is getting what it desires" — about as big a lie as you could publicly commit to, considering the town board's repressive acts against Lansing's unrepresented and unilaterally targeted rural community.

It's only fitting, after telling such a bald-faced lie, that their form-based section ends with a disclaimer, "The best way to plan for the long-term future of the Town of Lansing is to decide regionally." Lansing's form-based future is a comprehensive plan corruption that takes from those who have the least to benefit those who have the most — Cornell.

"Complete" Rubbish

Cornell Design Connect's "Complete Streets" is a transportation "design intervention" that drops the traffic and aesthetics of a "mini-city" bedroom community into the middle of a green rural landscape.

Design Connect's "best planning practices" not only accept the existence of major urban sprawl developments in a rural town; they're advocating "changes to town policy and planning procedure" to greatly increase its size and density through "urban design overlay zones." They recommend that the town "increase density and provide affordable housing," change zoning with "reduced minimum open space requirements," "density bonuses," and "amended density requirements," and build a new infrastructure to accommodate that increase. They merely tack the goals of efficiency and low carbon emissions onto what is clearly not the "best planning practice" for a rural community.

Their recommendations for Lansing include the "redevelopment of underutilized properties," while at the same time, there are block after block of old wood-frame houses downtown in the City of Ithaca that would be perfect sites for redevelopment as high-density housing, and thousands of unused acres suitable for building in the Town of Ithaca, surrounding the city's core.

The redevelopment of Ithaca's unused and underutilized building lots and the creation of affordable and appropriate urban housing would solve the housing shortage, require no new infrastructures, efficiently use existing bus routes, increase access to the cultural center of the county, have the highest possible walkability and greatest alternative transport choices for residents, and be in the closest proximity to jobs in the education, business, institutional, and health care sectors while minimizing the carbon footprint for transportation.

It would solve every one of Tompkins County's housing and transportation problems but one: it's a solution that Cornell does not want.

Everywhere, there is the exhortation for more and higher-density housing in the Town of Lansing: high-density housing for affordable housing, high-density housing for sustainability, high-density housing for the environment, high-density housing for lower taxes, for the aging, for reducing carbon emissions, for curing cancer, for bringing about world peace. The high-density housing that Cornell plans for rural Lansing to maintain Ithaca's gentrified, college-town lifestyle for students and professors.

Cornell's Complete Streets design intervention takes a child's puzzle-book approach to solving the real-world problems of urbanizing traffic by ignoring the practical consequences inherent in high-volume, slow-moving traffic: people will look for ways to avoid it.

Lansingville Road is a twenty-foot-wide rural roadway that has seen a great increase in through-cutting traffic in recent years: cars, trucks, even commercial tractor trailers and flammable liquid trucks speed down the middle of the road and routinely pass on the double yellow line. Lansingville Road is now becoming recommended by Google Maps as a quicker route than the state highway, but authorities still refuse to impose speed limits, give out tickets, or even admit that there is a problem.

Tompkins County claims that they don't have the money for traffic control in rural Lansing — but they do have the money to re-pave Lansingville Road this year, further incentivizing its use as a no-law-enforcement traffic corridor through a poor rural community.

Cornell's Complete Streets for the Town of Lansing represents yet another poorly thought-out solution with a well thought-out agenda — Cornell's expansion and profit.

NYSDEC + TMDL = Business as Usual

You're the New York State Department of Environmental Conservation (NYSDEC), and you're responsible for a program to clean up nutrient pollution in Cayuga Lake.

You need to establish a Total Maximum Daily Load (TMDL): the maximum amount of a pollutant that a waterbody can accept and still meet the state's water quality standards. But your own studies show that agricultural activities are responsible for more than four times the phosphorous pollution of all the other polluting sources combined — and the agricultural lobby has immense political power.

So you give Cornell — a land-grant university with a college of agriculture — the authority "to fund and manage a monitoring and modeling program with NYSDEC oversight."

How well did this work?

Press release: "DEC Proposes New Phosphorus Limits to Protect Cayuga Lake Water Quality. . . . Phosphorus comes from facilities that include wastewater treatment plants, municipal separate storm sewer systems, agricultural runoff, and other sources."

Since the NYSDEC mentions agriculture last, it's not too hard to figure out.

All Roads Lead to Cornell

While you may question the motives for a county official's actions, you know that they're never acting alone — and always in the best interests of Cornell.

The following is an example of how the government operates.

Our rural road became a shortcut for commercial and industrial traffic avoiding the state highways. Some days, a couple of hundred gravel trucks alone would barrel down the middle of its twenty-foot-wide strip of asphalt. We asked our county legislator for a four-ton limit on "through haul trucks" (something that is commonly done on the smaller connecting roads in Cornell's nearby bedroom community).

This is the county highway director's reply:

"Couple of quick thoughts: Trucks using this road are likely Agriculture or local and there would be no way of limiting either. If they are Through Haul Trucks I don't understand why they would be using this road? Do you know of any reason?"

The first roadblocks of bureaucratic denial: 1) You don't recognize what they are. 2) You don't understand the law. 3) Why would anybody do this?

Not only are agricultural vehicles familiar, the gravel trucks are filled with gravel and emblazoned with the names of gravel-hauling companies, and "local delivery" means you're delivering, not driving through. And asking for a "reason" is as relevant as asking about the motivation for a drunk driver being drunk.

But these were just knee-jerk responses. When we informed him that we understood the situation and again pressed for a four-ton through haul weight limit, he responded:

"I have researched the area and talked to highway officials in Lansing and they report there are no large through haul trucks utilizing Lansingville Road. What is using the road is as I thought, Agriculture Vehicles."

The only answer to this outrageous statement was to send photographic evidence of these trucks, which we did. There was no response, ever.

Sometime later, a sign suddenly appeared on our road: "Weight Limit 20 Tons – Except Local Delivery."

This is five times the weight limit of every other through-haul weight limit sign I have seen on any road in the county.

Then I noticed the same sign posted on a nearby rural road: a hilly, winding 25 mph road that connects the state highway with the same state highway along a longer and much more time-consuming route. An unnecessary and unasked-for sign, posted to pretend that we were not the sole target.

Our county legislator had already faded into the "hands-off" distance, so I put the matter before the County Ethics Advisory Board, enumerating the highway director's puzzling conduct and public denial of the facts. With college town cleverness, they came back at me sideways, ignoring the substance of my letter and responding that the highway director "posted the road at 20 tons to limit through traffic of large trucks."

When I wrote back that this in no way responded to my complaint, they ceased all communication.

You could put "Misconduct" on a billboard, and no county authority would admit to noticing it.

This is only the beginning of a runaround that has gone on for years: the progress-less treadmill of rural participation. Cornell's policymakers do whatever they decide to do, and they've already decided that rural people are usable and disposable.

Rural Road Trip

Our rural road woes are not limited to through haul trucks.

Drivers routinely pass on the double yellow line, and big trucks drive on whatever side of the road is convenient for taking the curves at speed.

Twice in four years, Medevac helicopters landed in my front yard to airlift road accident victims.

We have been refused any sheriff's patrols or traffic enforcement, or even any official acknowledgment that there is a problem.

Our county legislator and the town's deputy supervisor said that we would gain their support with a petition. After we went door to door for signatures, 95% of the residents signed its request for a 40 mph speed limit on our unposted 4.8-mile rural road.

Afterwards, neither the legislator nor the deputy supervisor would sign or support the petition, and both stopped all further communication.

The NYSDOT's adjudication of our petition gave us a mocking 50 mph speed limit posting for just six-tenths of a mile through the center of our hamlet — in contrast to miles of state and county highways all around us with speed limits of 45, 40, and even 35 mph.

Persevering, we used a webcam and recognition software, compiling data that showed a 40 mph average speed and 45 mph 85th percentile, and gathered more research material, including screen shots documenting the disturbing fact that Google Maps is now recommending our road as a quicker route than the state highway a mile away.

This evidence was emailed to the planners and officials involved at the local, county, and state levels, asking for their support for a 45 mph speed limit in compliance with 85th percentile "best practices," and noting the seriousness of the ongoing rerouting of highway traffic.

The county's highway director replied:

"I feel I can speak for everyone that our show of support for a reduction comes in the manner of submitting a request to the state for those purposes."

It's one of the defining features of our collegiate-run government that officials have such an educated way of telling the rural residents, "You can go f**k yourself."

Our new town supervisor took a month to reply that they would discuss the possibility of supporting our request at a town board meeting — in another five weeks. Here we go again.

We were ready to present our case at that meeting but were told that the agenda had filled up, and we were bumped to the next monthly meeting.

At that meeting, we were finally able to give a PowerPoint presentation of photos and charts to document our requests to the town board. There were a couple of other presenters, one of whom wanted to name a local bridge that had been rebuilt.

The next meeting's minutes had no mention of our road but detailed at length the board's approval of the name for the rebuilt bridge.

To the Town of Lansing government, the safety and welfare of the rural community is less important than naming a bridge to create a historical context that never existed and satisfy a suburban pastiche of reimagined rural icons.

While everyone in government repeatedly tells us what we need to do, no one has actually stepped up to do anything or even admitted that we have a problem. Instead, they keep passing us on to another group, who in turn pass us on to another.

It's local, county, and state authorities performing in a three-act farce, spinning, allotting, and killing the hopes of rural residents. Tompkins County's rural community is never helped or supported by Cornell's policymakers. Instead, we're constantly reminded that we need to follow the proper procedure in the hopes of meeting conditions that can never be met.

In 1981, noted anthropologist Janet Fitchen wrote about rural New York:

"The real tragedy of these small enclaves of marginality and poverty is that people are playing a game of life that has been structured in such a way that they are required to play but prevented from winning."

It's an inequity that still exists. The only change is that the colleges that traditionally ignored our rural poverty and marginalization are now taking advantage of it.

Deadly Drift

No matter how hard I've tried to bring the conditions of those living in rural Tomkins County to the attention of a wider audience, it never seems to work out. But while the public may be uninformed, authorities have a clear picture of the continued abuse and marginalization of our rural communities. They should, since they're the source of it.

Rural people are the "go-to" sacrifice for politicians and bureaucrats at all levels of government. The rural community is so powerless, and its issues so unreported, that every choice — from covering up CAFOs to blatantly inequitable policymaking — is a no-brainer for ensuring career longevity and re-election.

Rural governance is a recirculating pump that puts rural abuse through an endless loop of delays and denials. Here's how it works:

I was mowing my lawn on a windy day when an agricultural boom sprayer drove up to me, engulfing me in a large cloud of Roundup. I quickly went inside and cleaned up, but I had breathed quite a bit in before I could escape.

Immediately after the occurrence, I reported this incident to the agribusiness that sprayed me, but they didn't even offer an apology.

That night, I became dimly conscious that I was standing in the middle of the bathroom, vomiting all over myself and the floor and the toilet, and I didn't even care. I crawled back into bed and stayed there for twenty-four hours. It took a full week for me to feel almost normal.

My complaint to the NYSDEC brought two investigators, and a report that needed a Freedom of Information Law (FOIL) request to see. The investigation blamed me. It was reported that I expressed opinions against farming, implied that I was either lying out of malice or had sprayed myself, and ended with "case closed!"

It is notable that the NYSDEC investigation into herbicide drift poisoning never provided any facts regarding the wind speed, wind direction, or application restrictions, and relied on assertions and suppositions to discredit my testimony and the incident itself.

I collected data from the National Oceanic and Atmospheric Administration (NOAA) showing local wind speeds of 16–17 mph, gusting to 23 mph during the time of the incident, and along with a review of the NYSDEC report by an expert investigator of wide experience (who was concerned about its lack of facts and the appearance of bias), sent them to state senators and representatives with copies of the original investigation and other reference material. Everything was passed back to the NYSDEC.

The regional director responded that the DEC had "reviewed this matter," "the initial investigation was thorough," and "the decision not to pursue administrative or criminal enforcement was proper." Again, they offered no facts of any sort.

Last year, I received a phone call from a former employee of that same agribusiness, stating that he had read my account of herbicide poisoning in "Cornithaca County" and that the company had instructed employees to spray in conditions that were "too hot and too windy" to comply with federal label application instructions.

I gathered this and all the other information and sent it to the New York State Attorney General's Office. They passed it all back to the NYSDEC. There has been no response.

Agricultural interests don't have regulators — they have friends.

Non-Disclosure Policy

If you would like an indisputable example of fraud, there is none better than the New York State Agricultural District Disclosure Form and Notice for ticking all the boxes.

In the United States, common law generally identifies nine elements needed to establish fraud: (1) a representation of fact, (2) its falsity, (3) its materiality, (4) the representer's knowledge of its falsity or ignorance of its truth, (5) the representer's intent that it should be acted upon by the person in the manner reasonably contemplated, (6) the injured party's ignorance of its falsity, (7) the injured party's reliance on its truth, (8) the injured party's right to rely thereon, and (9) the injured party's consequent and proximate injury.

The New York State Agricultural District Disclosure Form and Notice states:

"This disclosure notice is to inform prospective residents that the property they are about to acquire lies partially or wholly within an agricultural district and that farming activities occur within the district. Such farming activities may include, but are not limited to, activities that cause noise, dust and odors."

Let's examine a few of the activities that those "prospective residents" are not being fully informed of.

Satellite lagoons: "Lagoon" is a euphemism for an open cesspit (frequently a million gallons or more) of feces, urine, antibiotics, antibiotic-resistant bacteria, and toxic heavy metal that is sluiced from the floors of CAFO sheds and fermented for months before being sprayed on and injected into the earth. "Satellite" refers to the currently recommended practice of placing them far from the farm headquarters (i.e., close to the neighbors) for convenience of application. These cesspits emit toxic methane and hydrogen sulfide gases at levels that are only permissible in rural communities. The week after you buy your house, a farmer could build one in the field next door.

<u>Agricultural laws:</u> Prospective buyers are not informed of the legal ramifications of being a "non-farmer" under the state's agricultural laws.

"The Agricultural Districts Law authorizes the Commissioner to issue opinions, upon request, concerning the soundness of specific agricultural practices. If the Commissioner determines that a practice is sound, the practice shall not constitute a private nuisance."

"Article 25AA of New York State Agriculture and Markets law includes a Right To Farm provision which requires the Commissioner of Agriculture and Markets to resolve disputes about farm practices on farm operations within agriculture districts."

Simply put, all farmer vs. non-farmer disputes are adjudicated by, and for the benefit of, farming interests.

<u>Health hazards:</u> In finding against plaintiffs suffering from the effects of manure off-gassing that included brain damage in one child and the surgical removal of eyelids in an adult, the United States Court of Appeals for the Second Circuit (Mather v. Willet

Dairy), commented that agricultural laws "may be inadequate for ensuring the safety of our environment and for protecting citizens from serious injury. But that is the remedy that Congress has provided and to which we are bound."

From the National Library of Medicine: *Exposure to concentrated animal feeding operations (CAFOs) and risk of mortality in North Carolina, USA*

"Highlights:

- Presence of CAFOs was associated with higher risk of mortality.
- People living near CAFOs had significantly higher risk of cardiovascular mortality than other persons.
- We found an increasing trend of higher risk of cardiovascular mortality with higher levels of CAFOs exposure.
- Findings have implications for future studies of environmental justice and CAFOs."

And in the conclusion:

"Our study adds to the literature on health outcomes associated with CAFOs, indicating that proximity to these facilities increases risk of mortality."

And from my own experience of being sprayed with Roundup by an agricultural boom sprayer while mowing my lawn: Prospective buyers should be informed that they have no legal protection for the health of their families, even where there are laws.

<u>Removal of previously permitted land uses:</u> As demonstrated by the recent Lansing Town Board's creation of an agricultural zone, any rural permitted uses (even those permitted as of right) can be stripped from rural residents, summarily removing the uses that the purchaser originally bought the land for.

The New York State Agriculture Disclosure Statement is usually handed to prospective purchasers at the closing, where its uninformative wording will not cause them to back out at this psychological moment, and leaving them no time for thought or investigation.

My attempts to persuade New York State to create an Ag Disclosure Statement that accurately disclosed the possible hazards of purchasing property in an agricultural district have all been a complete failure.

When I approached Tompkins County legislators, urging them to supplement the NYS Ag Disclosure with a more purchaser-friendly county disclosure statement, they also refused, stating that it was the local Board of Realtors and the County Agriculture and Farm Protection Committee who were the "stakeholders."

The New York State Agricultural Disclosure Statement is the perfect legal instrument for protecting those who fraudulently profit from the ignorance of others.

More importantly, if you were to dig down through all this misconduct to the underlying cause — the root cause of every rural policy and act — you would find that it's not about agriculture at all. It's about money.

Politicians and corporate agribusiness have created a fog of "agriculture" in rural New York to hide the manifest injustice that takes place within it. The agriculture lobby represents the most politically powerful and privileged group in the country, and the rural population is the most unrepresented and marginalized sector of the nation's poor.

That makes rural people easily disposable. And when you're disposable, you can't be the victim of anything — even of fraud.

Runaround

My attempts to change the fraudulent New York State Agricultural District Form and Notice are going nowhere, because there's nowhere to go.

The most interesting aspect of New York's rural policies is not the lack of public participation, but how this is accomplished.

Progress is derailed by broken promises, and communication is halted by mirror-like interfaces that merely stare back at those who attempt to use them.

Public participation is only bureaucratic form filling with no place for your questions, and politicians gauge your satisfaction with no concern for your reasons.

Every telephone menu is filled with drawn-out explanations of why you shouldn't and don't need to speak to anyone, and persisting eventually leads to a barely intelligible voice, always ending with "leave a message . . . leave a message . . . leave a message . . ." It's like standing on the shore of an uncaring sea talking to the waves, never receiving a reply to break the monotony of empty expectations.

I have already spent hours and days in the well-worn paths of participatory door knocking.

I have caught a few by surprise, but they always recover and send me on to the appropriate dead end.

Every open door leads to a closed one.

Every source of help or adjudication is unwilling, unable, or uninterested.

Their lack of response is an uncaring that results from caring more for everything else. An uncaring that finds no use for us as anything but disposable. We are living in the second generation of "the greater good," a presumptuous importance that allows any act to be excused.

Just as in Tompkins County's "progressive" planning vision, there is no place for rural values and communities in our city-centric future — unplanned differences are not allowed.

The journey of rural public participation goes nowhere. It starts at the end of the line, leaving us waiting for a train that was derailed fifty years ago.

We have devolved into a society where equality and equitable treatment are so important that any evil used to achieve it can be excused, and yet, the most repressive and discriminatory policies against a poor, marginalized people can also be excused through that same belief in "importance." Good luck with that.

In Conclusion

The destruction and disappearance of our rural community continues unabated. Cornell is sloganizing, "Lansing is Leading the Way," but there is no other municipality that is following, and our leaders will decamp in the night as we approach our destination.

The *new* Town of Lansing has all the traditional values of a fast food breakfast menu, and all the future of food wrappers on the highway out of town.

In rural New York, no one can hear you scream.

Epilogue

All follow-up emails to our Town Board presentation requesting rural traffic control and enforcement have received no response or acknowledgement.

A seven-page letter detailing the fraudulent aspects of the Agricultural District Disclosure Form and Notice was sent to numerous politicians and the NYS Agriculture and Markets Commissioner. One State Senator passed it on to another Senator, who passed it on to the Agriculture and Markets Commissioner. There has been no additional action.

The Tompkins County Department of Assessment refuses to admit that there are negative impacts from any industrial farming activity.

Doug Baird

Lansingville, *July 4, 2024*